THIS BOOK CONTAINS THE TREASURED MEMORIES OF

_____

IN THE GIFT SHOP OF GRATITUDE

GIFT SHOP
of
GRATITUDE

*A Journal to Explore
the Journey of Your Life*

PETER LOVENHEIM
with a Meditation on Gratitude
by Rabbi David A. Katz

Published 2024 by Gildan Media LLC
aka G&D Media
www.GandDmedia.com

GIFT SHOP OF GRATITUDE. Copyright ©2024 by Peter Lovenheim. All rights reserved.

No part of this book may be used, reproduced or transmitted in any manner whatsoever, by any means (electronic, photocopying, recording, or otherwise), without the prior written permission of the author, except in the case of brief quotations embodied in critical articles and reviews. No liability is assumed with respect to the use of the information contained within. Although every precaution has been taken, the author and publisher assume no liability for errors or omissions. Neither is any liability assumed for damages resulting from the use of the information contained herein.

Front cover design by Tom McKeveny

Illustrations by David Rheinhardt of Pyrographx

Interior design by Meghan Day Healey of Story Horse, LLC

Library of Congress Cataloging-in-Publication Data is available upon request

ISBN: 978-1-7225-0695-7

10   9   8   7   6   5   4   3   2   1

Contents

Meditation on Gratitude by Rabbi David A. Katz   11
Welcome to the Gift Shop   15

1   Deck of Playing Cards:
     The Hearts We Hold Closest.................21

2   Bobbleheads:
     People on a Pedestal...................... 29

3   Snow Globes:
     Circling Your World 37

4   Coffee Mugs:
     Sip from the Cup of Wisdom.............. 45

5   Refrigerator Magnets:
     The Attraction of Travel................... 53

6   Scented Candles:
     Fragrant Memories 61

Contents

7 Toy Animals: Furry Friends and
Other Pets Who Touched Your Life....... 69

8 T-shirts:
Meaningful and Memorable Moments 77

9 Souvenir Spoons:
Meals to Remember 85

10 Bookmarks:
Words that Leave a Mark.................. 93

11 Baseball Caps:
Being Part of the Team 101

12 Music Boxes:
The Soundtrack of Your Life 109

13 Souvenir Pens:
Outlets for Self-Expression 117

14 Jewelry:
The Beauty Around Us....................125

15 Shot Glasses:
To Your Health! 133

16 Key Chains:
Opening Doors of Opportunity...........141

17 Jigsaw Puzzles:
For Life's Puzzling Choices 149

Contents

18 Ornaments:
Reminders of Faith and Ritual 157

19 Tote Bags:
The Things We Carry With Us 165

20 Postcards:
Glad I Was Here 173

Acknowledgments   181
About the Author   185

Für Elisa

Meditation on Gratitude

"Who is rich? Those who rejoice in their lot."
—Simeon Ben Zoma (Babylonian Talmud)

The great sage Ben Zoma's words ring true now more than ever. Getting what we want may be the key to happiness, but it is only a fleeting joy because, after getting what we want, we will want more.

This book will evoke memories for you of people and places and events. Appreciating what we presently have leads to lasting happiness because no matter how our fortunes may change, there is always something in our lives for which to give thanks.

Why is it so challenging to appreciate what we already have? The reasons are many. Madison Avenue turns us into constant consumers, and online shopping makes the whole world a marketplace. Even knowing that luck or fate may have dealt us a good hand, we are still blinded by belongings we think we deserve, so we begin to take for granted the gifts that fill our lives.

A sense of gratefulness may come not only by comparing our situation with others, but it may also come with proactive strategies that remind us to count our blessings. Some follow proscribed religious rites, rituals, or prayers to place into their mouth words of thanksgiving. Others utilize personal strategies such as daily journaling or mindful recitation.

Peter Lovenheim offers a highly original way to recognize the many gifts that are already ours. His starting point is a survey of items we find in an ordinary gift shop. He shows us how each one of these items can prompt us to reflect upon a gift we have received in life. Snow globes might remind us of natural wonders that have inspired us, toy animals may bring to mind a childhood pet we loved, jigsaw puzzles can make us remember personal problems we could only figure out by putting all the pieces together. For Lovenheim, the superficial paraphernalia found in gift shops leads him to an appreciation of the many experiences in life that enrich us and bring us joy.

This is a remarkable book because, as the reader, you will continue to add to the text by filling out the gratitude pages with your own reflections on your journey of life. This is not a book to just read. It is a book to savor, reflect, ponder, and contribute to.

Once completed, you may give this book to your family, or you could tuck it away in a drawer to keep adding the new gifts you receive. When times are difficult, you may find great comfort in your own words because the treasures found here will be a reminder of all that is good in your life.

If you have received this book as a gift, know that the giver meant it to be more than an obligatory transaction. The contents of the book will fill your head with curious details and facts about gift shop items but, more important, the essays will make you reflect upon the many gifts in life that have come your way. In today's society, when so many are seeking happiness by attempting to gain more and more, this book will make you appreciate how much you already have. As Ben Zoma suggests, and I paraphrase, let us rejoice in what we have.

May you see the world as a shop filled with gifts, and let each one fill your heart with joy.

—Rabbi David A. Katz
Member, Central Conference of American Rabbis

Welcome to the Gift Shop

On a recent trip to France, I visited many tourist sites—Monet's home and garden at Giverny, the Palais Garnier or opera in Paris, and the Palais des Popes in Avignon. One thing many tourist sites have in common, I discovered, was that once you get in, the only way out—*sortie*, in French—is through the gift shop.

That put me off a bit. I'm okay with gift shops; all over the world they stock similar items—playing cards, stuffed animals, scented candles, and the like. But making a visit to the gift shop compulsory—that seemed crass.

And yet, the more gift shops I visited—and the more I thought about them—I began to see in the requirement to "exit through the gift shop" an unexpected bit of wisdom.

It got me thinking about mortality. I'm in my seventieth year, and while these days that's not considered very old, it is certainly closer to dusk than dawn. Naturally, at times, I've found myself wondering how I'll manage the final exit.

Now, considering my French experience, I'm thinking I may just exit through the gift shop.

I don't mean buying stuff. As the saying goes, "A burial shroud has no pockets."

What I mean is that I'll try to focus on the gifts of life for which I'm most grateful, and, as a useful way to give these thoughts some order, I'll imagine them as standard items in a gift shop.

In my imaginary gift shop, for example, there's the usual deck of playing cards, but on the back of each card, instead of photos of famous people or landmarks, are images of the people I'm most grateful to have had in my life: two cards for my parents, one each for my brother and late sister, one for my wife, three for my kids, one for their mom, two for my sons-in-law, six for grandkids, and half a dozen for closest friends.

In my mind, I can flip through these cards, shuffle them, cut the deck, but on each one will be the face of a person whom I have felt blessed to have known.

Surely in your gift shop you'll be able to assign cards to a multitude of people in your life.

My gift shop also has stuffed animals: a big one for the tri-color collie of my childhood; a smaller one for the lovable Lab-dachshund mix—just eleven inches high—of my children's early years.

What fond remembrances do you have of that beloved cocker spaniel or tabby cat?

My gift shop has scented candles, too, but not of lavender, lemon, or rosemary. One is the sweet smell from childhood of autumn leaves burning at curbside. Two others evoke my dad: one, the aroma of tobacco from the pipe he smoked when I was young; the other, the smell of ink that would hit my nose the moment I entered his print shop. Perhaps you recall the smell of your home when Mom and Grandma were cooking on a special holiday, or the scent of the books in your grandfather's study where he smoked cigars.

Is there a gift shop anywhere without bobbleheads? In mine, they're of mentors, teachers, and coaches whom I've admired and who have guided me in work and in life—and a few others I could always count on simply for a smile or laugh. Who are those people for you?

My gift shop also has jigsaw puzzles but not of lovely landscapes or seascapes. Instead, these puzzles depict difficult situations— losses and assorted troubles, some of my own making—that in my life I had to work through and resolve. I include them because with hindsight we know that sometimes it's only through wrestling with the tough puzzles that we grow. I'll prompt you to think of your own defining moments.

So there's a brief introduction to my Gift Shop of Gratitude—the one through which I plan to exit.

When I first wrote about this idea of gift shops and gratitude, many people contacted me to say they'd like to make a Gift Shop of

Gratitude for themselves. That's why I wrote this book.

Here, you'll find twenty chapters, each one based on a different item that you can find in almost any gift shop in the world, from the Louvre to a truck stop on I-80. For each one, I've shared some facts that I associate with the item—people, places, and memories I'm grateful for. There's plenty of space for you to do the same, and to tell about each one.

My hope is that when you're done, you'll have created your own Gift Shop of Gratitude: a beautiful testament to all the goodness you were given in life, and a precious record to leave behind for those who love you.

1

Deck of Playing Cards: The Hearts We Hold Closest

At the gift shop at Monet's house and gardens in Giverny, France, I bought a deck of cards. On the back sides were color reproductions of fifty-two of Monet's most famous paintings.

This is typical for gift shop playing cards: on the backs, you'll almost always find images of the place you've just visited. If it's an art gallery, the cards will showcase the paintings and sculptures you saw. If it's a national park, cards will have images of waterfalls, mountains, and other scenery. If it's a major city, the backs of cards will show prominent buildings, statues, and other landmarks.

In mathematical terms, there's something almost miraculous about playing cards. I've read that from a deck of fifty-two an almost infinite number of possible permutations can be made. The actual number is an eight followed by sixty-seven zeros, which is said to be more than the number of atoms on Earth. That means that any randomly shuffled deck of cards has almost certainly never been seen before and will never be seen again.

With any deck of cards, we can enjoy lots of games—poker, bridge, whist, go fish, whatever is your favorite—do magic tricks, and even build card houses.

But we can also use playing cards in another way: to remember the people we are most grateful to have had in our lives. For this reason, cards may be the most important item in the gift shop; it's why I put them first.

As I noted earlier, in my Gift Shop of Gratitude I'll have a deck of cards, but on the backs of each, instead of photos of famous people or landmarks, will be images of the people I hold dearest: two cards for my parents, one each for my brother and late sister, one for my wife, three for my kids, one for their mom, two for my sons-in-law, six for grandkids, and half a dozen for closest friends.

Who will be on your deck of cards?

You likely won't need all fifty-two cards (but lucky for you if you do!). Truth be told, we live in a disconnected time when, partly due to living so much of our lives online and partly because of the fracturing of families and ease of travel, many people report having only two or three people they feel close to and confide in. And yet, if you think of the full course of your life, there are likely many more people along the way whom you feel grateful to have known. These are people you've loved and who have loved you, whom you've cared about, and who have cared about you.

For starters, think of children, parents, grandparents, great-grandparents, brothers, sisters, aunts, uncles, cousins, stepfamily members, spouses, partners, first loves, friends, clergy, neighbors, military buddies, and others who come to mind.

As you flip through these cards, on each one will be the face of a person you feel blessed to have known. Shuffle the deck any way you like; they'll all be there—a unique collection of faces and remembrances, a testament to a lifetime of love and caring that you can hold in one hand.

Use the following pages to name the people in your deck of cards—the hearts you hold dearest.

Gratitude

Gratitude

Gratitude

2

Bobbleheads: People on a Pedestal

Bobbleheads in gift shops often reflect their locations. In London gift shops, bobbleheads are of the King, the Royal family, and the Beatles. In Las Vegas, they are of Elvis and other entertainers. Come to Washington, DC, and many of the oversized heads you'll see dancing atop springs are those of presidents—current, former, and wannabe. It makes sense, therefore, that the bobbleheads in your Gift Shop of Gratitude will be specific to your own life.

But who are good candidates for your personal bobblehead collection?

People collect bobbleheads of public figures they admire. So why not count among your bobbleheads someone you've admired: a mentor, teacher, or coach, or—since bobbleheads are amusing—maybe someone you've counted on for a smile or a laugh?

I don't think people would object to being bobbleheads. It's a bit cartoonish to see a big plastic head wobbling on a spring, but it turns out that bobbleheads have a long and distinguished background.

Historians trace bobbleheads back many centuries to a native art form in India. Made from clay or wood, these "head-shaking dolls" were painted in bright colors and dressed in fancy clothes. By the 1700s, Chinese artisans were making their own "nodding-head" figurines. Some were exported to the West. In England, the Prince of Wales (later George IV) acquired some and displayed them at his residence.

By the 1800s, bobbleheads made of porcelain were being produced in the US in limited quantities. The first bobbleheads made of plastic appeared in the 1950s. Bobbleheads of athletes, cartoon characters, and figures from popular culture became widespread. A complete set of Beatles bobbleheads is still a valuable collector's item.

By the first decade of the 2000s, you could buy bobbleheads of Albert Einstein, Nelson Mandela, and Justices of the Supreme Court. In 2019, the National Bobblehead Hall of Fame and Museum opened in Milwaukee, Wisconsin. The museum displays 6,500 unique bobbleheads—

the largest public display in history—and more than 500 bobbleheads are available for purchase in, of course, the gift shop.

In my Gift Shop of Gratitude, I'll have bobbleheads of people I admire for how they helped me along the way. The first are teachers: Clayton "Bud" O'Dell, who encouraged me to question and, by his example, inspired me to do my best; and Elizabeth Hart, who taught that writing is a craft and that with practice and hard work, it can be learned. Next is someone I met while writing a book: Dr. Louis Guzzetta. A retired surgeon who lived alone after his children were grown and his wife had died, Dr. Guzzetta taught me about living with loss and carrying on. Also, Jan Goldberg, a coworker and friend. Jan was steady under pressure and showed me how, when necessary, to "take a bullet" for the team. If Jan knew I was making him a bobblehead, I'm pretty sure he'd reply with one of his favorite lines, "Well, it's better than a poke in the eye with a sharp stick."

Finally, I'd give a bobblehead to any of several comedians whose work over the years has always made me laugh: George Carlin, Alan King, and Jerry Seinfeld.

Bobbleheads

Whom will you honor with a bobblehead?

If a teacher, remember it could be from a class other than academics: music, art, physical education, or shop. Or maybe it was an athletic coach whose attention and guidance were transformative.

Fill in the names of those you're honoring with bobbleheads and describe the relationship.

Gratitude

Gratitude

Gratitude

3

Snow Globes: Circling Your World

I love watching my grandchildren play with snow globes. No matter how much time they've spent watching television or staring at screens, there's something that seems to especially delight them about holding that transparent sphere and turning it over to watch the snow and glitter fall. I think it may make a child feel momentarily powerful: to hold a whole, tiny world in your hand, turn it upside down to make it snow, and then watch as snowflakes cover everything inside.

Nearly every gift shop in the world stocks snow globes. Most show famous local landmarks, some feature the built environment: Eiffel Tower, Empire State Building, Sydney Opera House; and some show natural beauty: a Saharan oasis, a Pacific coral reef, a snow-capped mountain. The irony of snow falling on a coral reef is puzzling yet fascinating. Whatever the scene, globes make popular souvenirs.

Their small size and light weight make them easy to travel with, and they're also easy to display at home on a bookshelf or mantel.

My favorites are snow globes with scenes of nature. They remind me of miniature versions of simple but special outdoor moments I've had and for which I'm grateful.

The story of how snow globes were invented is itself delightful. While there were types of snow globes around in the late 1800s, the first patent for one was issued in Vienna to Erwin Perzy, a mechanic who made surgical instruments. Perzy had been working to improve a type of lighting then used in operating rooms—a glass globe filled with water through which light could pass.

Other experimenters had filled the globes with ground glass to increase brightness, but Perzy had another idea for the filler: semolina, a hard grain. The semolina didn't increase brightness but, as the grain sank in the globe, Perzy saw that it created the pleasant appearance of snow falling. As it happened, he'd also just crafted for a friend a miniature cathedral out of pewter, and when he put this inside the snowy globe—voilà! The *Schneekugel*, the Viennese snow globe, was born.

Perzy was issued a patent in 1900. The company he later founded, Original Vienna Snow Globes, is still running and is now headed by a grandson. It exports hand-painted and hand-assembled snow globes—still made with real glass, not plastic—around the world. Not long ago, the company made globes for the children of US President Barack Obama.

In my gift shop, I'll stock snow globes that re-create in miniature three natural scenes I've most enjoyed and been grateful to have experienced. And just for fun, I'll imagine myself inside the globe.

The first will be an outdoor winter scene. In it, I'll walk in a silent wood in fresh-falling snow, the only sound the crunch of my footsteps.

The second will show a freshwater lake, maybe one of the Finger Lakes of central New York State near where I was raised. I'll swim there, floating on my back, watching puffy clouds go by.

My third globe will be of the Atlantic Ocean at sunrise. I'll stand on the shore, face the far horizon, and marvel to see the sun, like a giant red ball, rise god-like from the water.

What are the snow globe scenes that evoke the natural beauty and cherished experiences in nature you are most grateful for?

Gratitude

Gratitude

Gratitude

4

Coffee Mugs: Sips from the Cup of Wisdom

*A*pparently, Socrates, the ancient Greek philosopher, once said, "The only true wisdom is knowing you know nothing." I only know this because I saw it printed on the side of a friend's coffee mug.

Exactly when coffee mugs became a favored medium for expressing wisdom, I don't know, but I'm glad they did. I'm grateful for bits of wisdom wherever they're found. That's why I include coffee mugs—common in any gift shop—in my Gift Shop of Gratitude.

Of course, not everything printed on a coffee mug is profound, or even repeatable. And yet, even some amusing but less-than-profound quotes can contain a nugget of truth. I saw a mug recently that said, "OMG. My mother was right about everything!"

At their best, wise sayings—call them precepts, maxims, or aphorisms—can inspire and guide us in the face of life's uncertainties, dangers, and temptations.

Long before people displayed words of wisdom on their coffee mugs, they made sure their children learned them at school. Up until about a hundred years ago, children were taught penmanship by use of what were called copybooks. At the top of each page was printed a saying—maybe "If wishes were horses, beggars would ride," or "All that glitters is not gold"—and the child would copy it out line by line down the page until the penmanship was correct or at last more clear. In the process, the hope was that the child would learn and internalize the saying itself.

Rudyard Kipling's twentieth-century poem, "The Gods of the Copybook Headings," memorialized the lessons known at the time to millions of children.

Copybooks went out of fashion long before I started school, but my parents—who had been raised on such maxims—passed along many of their favorites to my siblings and me. I found them helpful over the years—although, even so, I've made my share of unforced errors.

When my kids were little, we shared maxims with them, sometimes framing favorite ones for display in the kitchen or study. Sometimes now when my adult children repeat some of these sayings, I know they've stayed with them, and it makes me smile.

In my gift shop, I imagine a row of coffee mugs displayed on a shelf with each one carrying one of the maxims that, over the years, I've found most helpful. Two are among those my dad taught me: one about choosing friends wisely, "Run with dogs and you'll get fleas," and another about worrying too much about the future, "Today's the tomorrow we worried about yesterday, and all is well." Two others are from those I shared with my kids: one about friendship, "To have a friend you've got to be a friend," and another about persistence, "Character is what you do on the second, third, and fourth try."

What sayings or expressions over the years have inspired and helped guide you? Did your parents teach them to you when you were young? Or, perhaps, did you find them on someone else's coffee mug? Or in a Chinese fortune cookie? Did you teach them to your children? In your gift shop, line up some coffee mugs and print them with some words of wisdom worth sharing.

Gratitude

Gratitude

Gratitude

5

Refrigerator Magnets: The Attraction of Travel

*M*igratory birds use the earth's magnetic field to guide them where they're going. We humans, on the other hand, use actual magnets to remind us of where we've been. I refer to souvenir magnets—those universal gift shop items that depict in images or words the different places we've traveled.

Souvenir magnets come in the shapes of all fifty states, the Statue of Liberty, Mount Rushmore, or the US Capitol. Abroad, you can find them in the form of the Eiffel Tower, the Leaning Tower of Pisa, the Pyramids of Egypt, a Scottish bagpiper, or a Dutch boy and girl in wooden shoes. Some magnets just spell out place names in colorful letters: "Barcelona," "Boston," "Las Vegas!"

It's probably not by accident that we put these reminders of adventure and travel in a place like the kitchen because the refrigerator is at the very center of a home. Like the dual notion of yin and yang in Chinese philosophy, "home" and "travel" are opposites and yet fit together. Home symbolizes security and travel offers adventure—yet both are, for many people, necessary parts of a satisfying life.

Sometimes, to be sure, as the innkeeper Thenardier in *Les Misérables* proclaims, "Travel's a curse!" There are missed connections, sudden illnesses, tourist traps, and other rip-offs. And yet, at its best, travel enriches our lives because we meet new people and consider intriguing ideas and are exposed to the wonders of the world, both natural and human-made. By placing these magnets in the very center of our homes, we're able to recall these enriching travels daily.

It's to the best of these travel experiences that we offer a place in our Gift Shop of Gratitude.

I recall with gratitude a road trip through the American Southwest with my college-age daughter, Valerie, including a tour of the seldom-visited Very Large Array, a radio astronomy observatory in central New Mexico and a key site on Earth from which humans explore the universe. Also, a tour with my wife of the Normandy beaches in France, the site of the World War II D-Day landings, and the beginning of the liberation of Western Europe from Nazi Germany. To see firsthand the wide beaches and steep cliffs where Allied soldiers gave their lives, and to walk in cemeteries among row upon row of grave markers, fills one with more gratitude than could fit in a hundred books.

If you could put souvenir travel magnets on a refrigerator in your Gift Shop of Gratitude, what travels and adventures would they recall? Some might be foreign trips to exotic places; some might be travels or even day trips closer to home. Either way, they're the kinds of experiences that pull us out of our daily routines and expose us to new people, places, and ideas, and, in so doing, enrich our lives.

Gratitude

Gratitude

Gratitude

6

Scented Candles: Fragrant Memories

People have used candles for thousands of years, but it was only in the second half of the twentieth century that their popularity as gift items soared.

The gifting began in 1969 in New Hampshire when sixteen-year-old Mike Kittredge discovered he didn't have enough money to buy a Christmas gift for his mother. So he melted some crayons to make her a candle. A neighbor saw what Kittredge had made and convinced him to sell her the candle. Kittredge took the money and bought more crayons—enough to make two candles: one for his mom and another to sell.

Thus was born a business that became the Yankee Candle Company. Five years later, when the company began selling scented candles, business took off. From one small shop, Yankee Candle expanded to hundreds of retail stores and then to over 35,000 authorized retailers worldwide. In 1998, Yankee Candle was sold to a private firm for $500 million.

Today, scented candles are everywhere. In the US, the National Candle Association estimates that one billion pounds of wax are used each year to make roughly four million candles. Among the places candles are most often bought are gift shops. Popular scents include vanilla, citrus, lavender, peppermint, and pumpkin. An estimated 10,000 different candle scents are now available.

Why are scented candles so popular?

Just lighting one engages four of our five senses: we hear the match scrape against a matchbox's striking surface; we see the flame rise on the wick; we feel the heat; then we smell the pleasant aroma of fragrant oils.

Smell is such a powerful sense, biologists say, in part because the olfactory nerves connect directly to a part of our brains related to emotion and memory.

It's natural, therefore, that many of the odors we best remember are those from early childhood. Mine include the sweet smell of autumn leaves burning at curbside. After a spectacular color show, our towering maples shed their orange and red leaves. Of course, I helped rake them into piles for burning (but not before jumping into a crisp pile).

Burning leaves in public was outlawed in my town in the early 1960s—so the last time I likely smelled that memory was nearly sixty-five years ago, at age eight or nine. And yet, the smell of autumn stays with me.

Some of our pleasure in scented candles may be for the scent itself—like those sweet burning leaves—but more often it is for the memories that the scent evokes.

In my Gift Shop of Gratitude, I'll have three candles. One with the scent of burning autumn leaves. The other two will evoke memories of my dad: one with the aroma of tobacco from the pipe he smoked when I was young; the other, the smell of ink that would hit my nose the moment I entered his print shop.

That last one—the smell of printer's ink—is especially powerful for me. Anytime I get a whiff of it—no matter how weak or fleeting—I'm instantly reminded of walking into my dad's print shop, hearing the giant presses pounding, seeing my dad in a white shirt seated at his desk, his sports coat hanging on a coat rack and papers covering his desk. That's just from a faint smell of ink.

Scented Candles

What scented candles will you stock in your Gift Shop of Gratitude?

Maybe smells of perfume that evoke a parent or other loved one? Or cooking odors from a childhood home or your own kitchen or from a favorite place to eat? Or backyard lilacs in bloom? Or the fresh smell of your baby just after a bath?

On the following pages, describe your candles' scents and what precious memories they help you recall.

Gratitude

Gratitude

Gratitude

7

Toy Animals: Furry Friends and Other Pets Who Touched Your Life

*T*oy animals—stuffed, carved, or sculpted—are common items in gift shops. Teddy bears are everywhere, but you also find animals specific to a region. In Casper, Wyoming, a gift shop I visited had buffalo; one near Miami had manatees. Recently, at a gift shop in Morocco, my wife bought a toy camel.

Toy animals remind us of the real animals we've cared for and loved—our pets and other animal companions. They deserve their own important place in the Gift Shop of Gratitude.

Surveys show that in the United States, about two-thirds of all households—that's nearly 90 million homes—include a pet, service animal, or other companion animal. Half of these homes have dogs and about a third have cats. During COVID, the demand for pets was said to have greatly increased, so these numbers are likely even higher now.

Living with animals, whether pets, service animals, or others, benefits people by increasing both physical activity and socialization, which can reduce anxiety, lower blood pressure, and reduce the risk of heart attacks. Dr. Edward Creagan of Mayo Clinic says these healing powers of pets are quite real and supported by scientific studies, but no one has to remind us of the joy we feel when we are greeted at the front door by a loving poodle or doodle or Lab. Children who grow up with pets tend to develop fewer allergies. Those are more than enough benefits, notes the Animal Health Foundation, to make up for chewed-up shoes, pooper scoopers, and hairballs.

I had two dogs, one when I was young and the other when my children were young.

Fella was a tri-color collie—black body, white mane, brown eyebrows and nose, and white paws. At a local breeder, my parents let me pick him out from a litter of puppies. I was three years old and chose him because he seemed the shyest. Fella and I grew up together. Well into my teens, he was a constant companion. I have a photo of him in his prime, lying in front of our house on the grass, white paws crossed, head erect, looking regal.

When my kids were little, we adopted Champ from the animal shelter. Champ was an unusual mix of black Lab and dachshund—he had the large head and tail of a Lab but stood only eleven inches high. Though he was small, Champ had a strong personality; among neighborhood dogs, he was the alpha male.

The time I lived with Fella and Champ was about twenty years in total. I came to love them both and I'm grateful I can make a place for each of them in my Gift Shop of Gratitude.

Have you had special pets or animal companions? They may have been dogs or cats, a favorite horse, a helpful, loving service animal, or even something exotic such as a cockatoo or clown fish or snake. Whoever they were, there's an important place for them in your gift shop. Write their names, maybe paste their photos, and tell about how you loved them.

 Gratitude

Gratitude

Gratitude

8

T-shirts: Meaningful and Memorable Moments

*N*ine in ten Americans surveyed say they own at least one T-shirt that they refuse to throw away because of sentimental reasons.

How does an inexpensive garment like a T-shirt—so named after the shape of its body and sleeves—become so valued?

To understand, let's first look at how T-shirts evolved from underwear to outerwear.

The T-shirt was born, say fashion historians, in the 1800s when American workers cut their one-piece "union suit" of long underwear in half to cope with the summer heat. Clothing companies began making T-shirts in the early 1900s, but the fashion got its first big boost in 1913 when the US Navy issued crew-necked white cotton undershirts to sailors. Some sailors—especially those serving in hot climates—removed their Navy jackets and instead wore just the undershirts.

Interestingly, the first appearance in print of the word *T-shirt* is said to have come in 1920 when F. Scott Fitzgerald, in his novel, *This Side of Paradise*, listed among the clothes packed by a college student "one sweater or T-shirt." (Today, perhaps tongue in cheek, Etsy vendors sell a T-shirt that says, suggestively, "I Want to F. Scott Fitzgerald.")

In the 1950s, when Marlon Brandon wore a T-shirt in *A Streetcar Named Desire* and James Dean wore one in *Rebel Without a Cause*, the T-shirt became a symbol of masculinity and rebellion. Then, in the 1960s and '70s, when screen printing on fabric became easier and cheaper—and of better quality—the T-shirt emerged as a space for images and slogans: a blank canvas for everything from corporate branding, band tours, and political statements.

From an item of fashion, the T-shirt became one of personal expression.

Today, T-shirts with pictures of tourist sites or that display clever sayings, including the classic: "My parents went to [Name of Vacation Spot] and All I Got was This Lousy T-shirt"—are found in gift shops worldwide.

But that still doesn't quite explain why nine of ten Americans won't part with a favorite T-shirt.

I should know; I have one. It sits in a cardboard box on the top shelf in a closet. It's forest green and in white block letters says: "Green Team, 1967." I wore it at age fourteen, the year at summer camp when I captained the winning color war team. I couldn't wear it now even if I wanted to: it hasn't fit me in more than fifty years. Why do I keep it? Because it's a tangible reminder of a happy, one-time experience. I'm sure my kids will toss it out when I'm gone, but for now, there it sits in a cardboard box.

It's an example of how something as simple as a T-shirt can hold memories of valued events, activities, or experiences. For this reason, the humble T-shirt deserves a place in our Gift Shop of Gratitude.

I've got another T-shirt too. It's dark blue and says, "Restore Balance to Brighton: Pat Reilly for Town Board." It's from a campaign I worked on for a friend running for local office. Pat didn't win, but the six months of campaigning was a rewarding time of creative work and camaraderie. Unless Pat runs again, I'm unlikely ever to wear the T-shirt, but I save it as a memento of a happy and meaningful experience.

T-shirts

Whether or not you hold on to a souvenir T-shirt, what are some of the treasured events, activities, and experiences that lent meaning to your life? Were you at Woodstock or another amazing concert? Did you attend a mass rally or work on a political campaign? Did your extended family hold a once-in-a-decade reunion—complete with custom-made matching family tees? Or the one from the bridal shower girls' trip to Vegas?

What would T-shirts in your Gift Shop of Gratitude say? Describe those meaningful and memorable moments.

 Gratitude

Gratitude

Gratitude

9

Souvenir Spoons: Meals to Remember

In 2023, it was reported that a woman from Davenport, Iowa, who had visited gift shops coast-to-coast and in twenty-nine countries, had amassed a collection of 8,500 souvenir spoons. She hoped to break the world record for the largest spoon collection.

Souvenir spoons, typically just over four inches in length, feature names or images of cities, states, countries, royalty, animals, and just about anything else you can think of. Historians trace their origin to a spoon made in the US in 1890 depicting George Washington. Soon after, as travelers here and in Europe began acquiring spoons marked with the names of places and famous landmarks, spoon collecting became an international craze.

Today, gift shops worldwide remain one of the principal places to find souvenir spoons as reminders of the places we visit.

But spoons—utensils for eating—can also serve to remind us of something special to be grateful for: memorable meals shared with family and friends. "Good food," it is said, "warms the heart and feeds the soul."

This is a tricky topic for me. I'm not what anyone would call a food connoisseur; I just never developed a strong appreciation for fine dining. But I certainly know others who have. My wife, for example, can recall first-rate meals from years ago, including all the portions and how they were arranged on a plate.

In contrast, my taste in food is pedestrian. I recall with gratitude, for example,
late-night dinners of hot meatball subs at an Italian diner in Boston. I was nineteen and one of a group of editors of our college paper, which was published daily. All evening and into the night we'd edit articles and design the paper and then, typically at about four in the morning, head over to the all-night diner. As we ate, we'd review the challenges we'd had getting out the next day's edition. Now, I marvel that I could even eat a meatball sub at four in the morning, let alone digest it, and then go back to my dorm and go to sleep.

Looking back, what I'm grateful for—more than the subs—was the companionship I enjoyed along with the meal. Not surprisingly, the word *companion* comes from *compaignon*, a word in Old French meaning "one who breaks bread with another."

I'm similarly grateful for the first meal I shared with my future wife. At a restaurant in Washington, DC, we ordered a cheese board—a variety of cheeses with crackers, dried and fresh fruits, bread, jam, and wine. Dinner lasted maybe two hours and by the time we finished, I think we both just understood that we were going to be a couple.

Another meal I'd include is any Sabbath dinner when my children were little. We'd light and bless the candles, the wine, and fresh challah bread (often homemade). I'd bless each of the children with the traditional Sabbath blessing, and then we'd enjoy an especially nice meal. Everyone would share in the conversation, and we'd end with some favorite songs. I know I've left out the part about the food, but it's what happened around the table that I most cherish, more than what was on the plate.

What are the meals you're most grateful for? Feel free to be more descriptive and appreciative of the actual food than I've been. Dig in.

Gratitude

Gratitude

 Gratitude

10

Bookmarks: Words that Leave a Mark

The oldest known bookmark, scholars say, was found in a book written by hand more than 1,500 years ago by Coptic Christians. It was discovered under the ruins of a monastery south of Cairo, along the Nile River. The bookmark, made of ornamented leather backed with vellum (calfskin), was attached by a leather strap to the sacred book.

That sounds like a serious bookmark.

Contemporary bookmarks have gotten a little more playful, like one I saw recently that says, "I FELL ASLEEP HERE" and another made so that the stockinged legs of the Wicked Witch of the East—complete with ruby slippers—stick up from the top of the book.

Bookmarks come in many varieties and are often among the least expensive items in a gift shop. Typically, you'll find bookmarks adorned with pictures of local landmarks, paintings from a local gallery, or a city's or town's name running vertically along its length.

Nowadays, the term *bookmark* can also mean a digital bookmark on which a web address can be stored for easy retrieval, but here I'm talking only of the physical kind.

Physical bookmarks remind us of something of immense value: the great books themselves that inform, entertain, comfort, and inspire. At its best, literature can impart insights and wisdom that may affect our view of the world and of life itself. Such works, and the authors who produce them, have a place in our Gift Shop of Gratitude.

My Gift Shop will include a nod to Thorton Wilder, author of the Pulitzer Prize-winning play, *Our Town*. I especially appreciate the scene in Act III where a young woman, Emily, who has just died in childbirth, receives permission to return to her previous life for one day only.

But which day? she wonders.

"Choose the least important day in your life," she's advised. "It will be important enough."

I first read that line more than half a century ago in high school, but I have "bookmarked" the passage, and its message is something I try to keep aware of daily.

Who are the authors and what are the written works that you've most appreciated over the years? They might be books, plays, or poems, but also articles, blogs, letters, or any other form of writing. Which are the ones that have most informed, touched, or influenced you? What have you bookmarked? Now it's your turn to write about them and give them a place in your Gift Shop of Gratitude.

Gratitude

Gratitude

Gratitude

11

Baseball Caps: Being Part of the Team

That friends of mine showed up at their wedding reception in matching "Bride" and "Groom" baseball caps suggests, I think, just how adaptable—and acceptable—classic American baseball caps have become.

Hundreds of millions of baseball caps are sold annually in the US, and many more millions abroad. They've become a playful platform to promote everything from sports teams to corporate logos, tourist sites, and political candidates. And they're worn with many different sports—not just baseball. Some police and members of the military wear them as part of official uniforms.

Lots of men who are balding—like me—wear them to look, well, less balding. Some women wear them on bad hair days with a ponytail swishing out the back.

Perhaps it's for all these reasons that in just about any gift shop—even in countries where most people don't know home plate from first base—you'll find baseball caps.

The traditional cap is made with a wide brim, some device in the back to adjust for size, six fabric panels to form the cap, and on top, a button. Originally used to help hold the fabric panels together, the button today is mostly decorative.

My collection of baseball caps is modest. One is from the Washington Nationals baseball club; another is from a company that sells bull semen (I visited there once while writing a book about dairy farming).

Baseball caps have a place in the Gift Shop of Gratitude because they reflect—and even promote—something essential to human happiness: being part of a group or team.

In one of the world's longest-running studies of adult life, researchers at Harvard found a strong correlation between people's flourishing lives and their satisfaction with relationships, including community relationships. In short, a sense of group belonging seems to be essential for human happiness.

The range of groups whose names, logos, and colors we may display on baseball caps is almost limitless. They include sports teams, schools and colleges, civic organizations, workplaces, branches of the military, and political parties.

Wearing a cap with a team or group name not only announces our affiliation but also fosters a connection with others who have the same affiliation. I'm reminded of when I first moved to Washington, DC. I knew almost no one in town. One day, while walking along a busy street, a man passing the other way stopped, said hello, and asked what year I'd graduated from college. For a moment I was puzzled, but then remembered I was wearing a cap with the name of my college's hockey team. We had a short chat and then went on our ways, but it was nice, even for just a moment, to feel connected.

What groups or organizations have you been part of that gave a meaningful sense of belonging? Maybe a sports team you played on or follow, your college alma mater, or a civic group like Rotary? Or an organization where you volunteered or to which you contributed financially? Or perhaps the branch of the military where you served, a company you helped build, or the place where you've worked for many years.

Here, give a shout out to the teams, groups, and organizations you're most grateful to have been a part of, and which, in turn, have given you a satisfying sense of belonging, so much so that you'd wear your affiliation on a baseball cap.

Gratitude

Gratitude

 Gratitude

12

Music Boxes: The Soundtrack of Your Life

*H*istorians generally agree that the first music box—with a revolving metal cylinder plucking flat metal prongs—was invented around 1770 in Switzerland by Antoine Favre-Salomon. A watchmaker, he was able to fit the entire mechanism inside a pocket watch.

Today, music boxes of various sizes and shapes—and which play a variety of tunes—can be found in many gift shops. The Seattle Opera gift shop, for example, sells a music box that plays Mozart's "Eine kleine Nachtmusik" (a little night music); and in St. Louis, at the Field Museum gift shop—located just across the street from Busch Stadium where the St. Louis Cardinals play—you can buy a music box that plays "Take Me Out to the Ballgame."

Other common songs played in music boxes include "You Are My Sunshine," "It's a Small World," and "Edelweiss." But caution: crank that little handle too much and with each of these catchy tunes you're in danger of infecting yourself with an earworm.

That's what happened when my wife and I visited the gift shop at the Avignon bridge in southern France. Music boxes sold there play the popular children's song, "Sur le Pont d'Avignon," which my wife recalled from middle school French class. It's a song ripe to become a melody that never ends, but I bought her the music box.

And I've still got the song in my head.

Music boxes remind us that music is something we can enjoy over a lifetime. Whether it's music we make ourselves, concerts we attend, or recorded music, taken together it all forms the soundtrack of our lives. A place in the Gift Shop of Gratitude is certainly due the talented people who compose and perform this music we cherish.

For me, this includes, in no particular order, Beethoven, the Beatles, the Beach Boys, and Joni Mitchell. Also, Patsy Cline, Rogers and Hammerstein, the musical *Les Misérables*, and Yip Harburg for all the clever song lyrics he wrote for *The Wizard of Oz*.

Thinking over the soundtrack of your life, what music has most touched, inspired, and comforted you? Who are the composers, performers, and songwriters you want to include in your Gift Shop of Gratitude? Sing their praises.

Gratitude

Gratitude

Gratitude

13

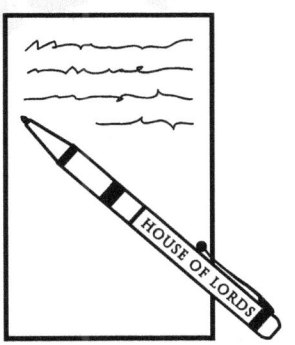

Souvenir Pens: Outlets for Self-Expression

The best pen I ever bought at a gift shop was one I found at the National Security Agency—the top US intelligence bureau—near Washington, DC. That a real-life spy outfit even has a gift shop surprised me.

They stocked the usuals: coffee mugs, shot glasses, key chains, and the like, but there were also clandestine types of trinkets such as spyglasses, fingerprint kits, and something called a "secret voice changer." But what caught my eye was a light-up pen. I suppose it was meant for snooping around in dark places, but I immediately saw it as a great writing tool. A pen with a light on the end would let me jot down notes in bed without having to switch on a bright night table light and fully wake myself up.

I bought the pen and have used it happily for years, always grateful to the National Security Agency.

I've bought pens at other gift shops, too, from a handsome, expensive red one I found at the House of Lords in London to a cheap one at a tourist gift shop in Washington, DC. I don't find any correlation between the price of a gift shop pen and the pen's quality as a writing tool. The cheap one from DC writes just as well as the costly one from the House of Lords.

(And, speaking of quality, the ink in the pens given away at my urologist's office doesn't flow well—an unfortunate reminder of why many people come to see a urologist in the first place.)

Nevertheless, there's always a place for pens in the Gift Shop of Gratitude because of what they represent: self-expression.

By self-expression I mean the expression of who we are—our personality, emotions, ideals, and opinions. Having some outlet for self-expression is essential for many people—and successfully finding that outlet is a reason for gratitude.

Often the outlet is through an artistic activity, but there are many variations. Consider whether some of these are among the ways you've found to express your authentic self.

Writing is a common form of self-expression. Books, articles, poems, journals, blogs, letters, song lyrics, and scripts for shows and podcasts are all forms of written self-expression.

Music is another, whether playing an instrument, singing in a chorus, or composing. A related form of self-expression is dance.

The visual arts, which include painting, drawing, sculpture, woodworking, ceramics, photography, video, and architecture, are also popular forms of self-expression. So is design, including graphic design, fashion design, and interior design.

Handicrafts, such as sewing, knitting, crochet, needlepoint, cross-stitching, calligraphy, felting, quilting, and weaving, are not only practical skills but also forms of self-expression. My grandmother, born in Vienna and an immigrant to this country as a young bride, made beautifully embroidered tablecloths and napkins. She's been gone a long time, but these expressions of who she was—a cultured, talented, hard-working woman—still adorn our family's holiday tables.

The culinary arts—cooking and food presentation—are other forms of expression. Time-tasted and time-honored recipes are handed down from generation to generation.

What are the ways you've found to express yourself? They deserve a place in your Gift Shop of Gratitude, so put pen to paper and tell about how you've learned to express yourself over the years.

Gratitude

Gratitude

Gratitude

14

Jewelry: The Beauty Around Us

*E*arrings, necklaces, pendants, bracelets, charms, rings, and lapel pins—you can find them all in display cases in many gift shops. Most are inexpensive costume jewelry, but some gift shops, such as those connected with top-rated museums, carry costlier pieces. Indigenous artisan silver and turquoise pieces, for example, can be found in gift shops in the Southwest.

That gift shops so often stock jewelry is a reminder that beautiful things—and beauty itself—can have a place in our Gift Shop of Gratitude.

What is beauty? Philosophers have long debated the question. Is it the perfection of form? Or, looked at another way, does it reflect life's impermanence and imperfection? Or should we say, in the words of the poet John Keats, "Beauty is truth, truth beauty"?

Fortunately, we needn't resolve the philosophical question. "Beauty is in the eye of the beholder" goes the proverb, and that will suffice.

Jewelry

Beauty, wherever we find it, is something to be grateful for.

There's the beauty we experience in nature: watching the sun rise over the ocean, looking at the sky on a cloudless, starry night, hiking a snow-capped peak, and seeing the Grand Canyon.

For me, I recall with gratitude a trip to Northern California and a morning spent walking among the giant redwoods.

There's also natural beauty that we experience closer to home: the sight of a cardinal at the window on a snowy winter morning; a spider's web with its intricate, mathematical design; and a golden maple leaf as it falls gently to the ground.

There's beauty that people create: a Beethoven symphony, Michelangelo's *Pieta,* the Taj Mahal. Gratitude for the chance to have heard or seen up close human-made wonders like these can have a place in our gift shop.

And then there's the beauty of those we love: the delicate softness of a baby's hand, a child's tight hug of a parent, the caring face of a loved one.

Even though I agree with the sentiment, "The most beautiful things in life are not things," it's also true that some things are, indeed, beautiful.

High-tech devices, for example, can be beautiful in design: Apple watches and other products come to mind. Larger items too: a finely crafted harpsichord, an elegantly designed racing bike, or a classic car.

Everyday household items of simple design—a bowl, a plate, or a teapot—can also be beautiful in craftsmanship and durability. They are constant companions: we see, touch, and use them daily as they accompany us through life.

The beauty we perceive in some items may grow the longer they're with us. Family heirlooms, for example—a pocket watch, a homemade quilt, the family Bible, a wooden bench crafted by an ancestor, or a piece of jewelry. We treasure these not so much as owners but as temporary custodians, as we pass them along the generations.

Where have you experienced beauty? Was it a part of the natural world seen in a far-away place, or something closer to home, even in your backyard? Are there beautiful objects you've had the privilege to see, or even to own?

They may be family keepsakes or just simple, well-made items used daily. Select a few of your favorites and create a beautiful place for them in your Gift Shop of Gratitude and tell their stories so generations to come can understand their history.

 Gratitude

Gratitude

 Gratitude

15

Shot Glasses: To Your Health!

While the word *shot* has been used to mean a drink of alcohol since at least the 1600s, the term *shot glass* is more modern, dating only to the mid-twentieth century. Before drinking from a shot glass, it's become a tradition to offer a toast. Typically, this is a wish for the good health and long life of one's drinking partners.

In English, we might say, "To your health!" The same toast is made in other languages: in Spanish, "Salud!" in French, "A votre sante!" in Arabic, "Fisehatak!" in Hebrew, "L' Chaim!" in Russian, "Na zdorovie!"

That most gift shops sell shot glasses, but not alcohol, may seem odd until you consider how small shot glasses are—most hold just 1.5 fluid ounces—how lightweight they are, and how inexpensive. All told, they make the ideal souvenir: easy on the wallet, easy to pack and transport, and, for some, a nice collectible.

Even with their small size, shot glasses can be decorated with place names or images of famous landmarks. I've got a shot glass that a friend brought me from a trip to Mexico. It's got a picture of a big orange sun against some palm trees, and in yellow block letters says, "PLAYA DEL CARMEN." A few years ago, my friend died suddenly. I think of him, of course, every time I use the glass.

Some shot glasses are printed with humorous sayings. One I saw proclaims "Hakuna MaVodka—It Means No Memories." Another says, "Alcohol: Because No Great Story Started over a Salad."

That shot glasses are so often used to toast good health makes them convenient reminders of something we're all grateful for: our health and those who help keep us well. These would include the doctors we see regularly, of course, but also surgeons, specialists, dentists, nurses, as well as therapists, pharmacists, nutritionists, and trainers who help us keep in shape.

In my Gift Shop of Gratitude, I'll include several doctors, from my childhood up to the present, who have been especially skillful, attentive, and kind. And though I don't recall her name, I'm also grateful to a young physical therapist who, after I'd broken my leg, taught me over many challenging weeks how to walk again.

Who has helped keep you healthy or helped you recover from some malady? In addition to doctors, nurses, and others, these angels might include aides who provided long-term care at a nursing facility or home, a hospice nurse when your mother was dying, a mental health therapist, or your family's own Dr. Marcus Welby who used to make house calls.

Here's the place to raise a glass to them in appreciation and thanks for good health, and to record their names in your Gift Shop of Gratitude.

Gratitude

Gratitude

Gratitude

16

Key Chains: Opening Doors of Opportunity

*I*n Austin, Texas, at the Texas Capitol Gift Shop, you can buy a key chain with a brown leather fob showing the state seal of Texas in gold-tone, for $6.

If your taste in key chains runs a little richer, try a brushed leather one with a metal Yves Saint Laurent signature. Online, it'll set you back only $265. And if that still leaves your house keys feeling underdressed, visit Prada online where a key chain in black Saffiano leather with an enameled, triangle-shaped charm—also available in orange, citron yellow, and mango—is yours for just $495.

If there's one item ubiquitous in gift shops, it's key chains. They're small, cheap—if you stay away from fashion designers—and practical. We've all got keys, and they all need a place to hang.

As it happens, my own most recent gift shop purchase was of a key chain. This occurred at the Wright Brothers National Memorial in Kitty Hawk, North Carolina. I didn't need a key chain—I already had one and, anyway, I have only three keys—but after touring the memorial I was filled with awe at the Wright brothers' achievement in flight, and the key chain's circular metal fob depicted a blue sky, the year 1903, and the Wrights' amazing plane on its first historic flight. For $6.95, why resist?

I'm not alone in the occasional urge to buy a souvenir key chain. They're a popular item for collectors. The current champion key chain collector, according to the *Guinness Book of World Records*, is Angel Alvarez Cornejo of Seville, Spain, whose collection consists of 62,257 items. Cornejo, who began collecting at age seven, stores his key chains in his garage and a rented warehouse.

But what do key chains have to do with the Gift Shop of Gratitude?

Keys open doors, and there may be doors to places so special that we want to remember them in our gift shop. This could include the door to your first home, to the apartment where your first child was born, or to a favorite vacation spot enjoyed by the family year after year.

But doors can also be metaphorical—as in "doors of opportunity." In this sense, we may owe a debt of gratitude to people who helped open important doors for us.

Some people may have helped us by opening career doors. These might have been teachers, mentors, career counselors, or older friends who made introductions and helped us land that all-important first job.

Other important doors may have led to a new spiritual path, a new subject of study, a new hobby or sport, or a new way to stay in shape or eat better. Some doors may have led us to a new business partner, a new friend, or the person we married.

My door openers include editors who helped me develop as a writer, a mentor who opened a door that led to a rewarding job, and a friend who opened several doors that led to other valued friendships.

Are there some physical places so special—such as first homes or vacation spots—that you want to remember in your gift shop? And who are the people who opened doors that led to some of the work, relationships, and experiences for which you're grateful? Here, name the door openers, and tell about some of the doors they helped open for you.

 Gratitude

Gratitude

Gratitude

17

Jigsaw Puzzles: For Life's Puzzling Choices

$\mathcal{F}$or nearly fifty years, my dad and uncles ran a printing company and one of the things they made were jigsaw puzzles. Growing up, I learned to appreciate a well-designed puzzle—and enjoyed an inexhaustible supply. That's why I'm always curious to check out the puzzles for sale at gift shops.

At the Museum of Fine Arts in Boston, for example, you can buy a 300-piece puzzle of an Edward Hopper seascape painting. Gettysburg National Military Park in Pennsylvania has a 750-piece puzzle that depicts Lincoln's Gettysburg Address. In Dearborn, Michigan, the Henry Ford Museum of American Innovation sells a 1,000-piece puzzle showing two dozen models of Ford cars and trucks.

During the COVID-19 lockdowns, the sale of puzzles soared. That's not surprising: they're an inexpensive, long-lasting, and even reusable form of entertainment. Nearly a hundred years earlier, during the Great Depression, puzzles also saw a jump in popularity.

Maybe it's because I grew up with them, but I've always seen jigsaw puzzles as a metaphor for real-life puzzles—the kind we didn't ask for and have no easy answers to, but that we must work through as best we can. And yet, once all the pieces of a real-life puzzle are in place, and we step back and see the picture we've created, often we're grateful for having met the challenge and come through it stronger, and maybe even wiser.

That's why I include puzzles in the Gift Shop of Gratitude.

The real-life puzzles I'm thinking of take many forms. Some involve a falling out with friends, changes in a career path, challenges of keeping a marriage on track, or coping with illness and loss.

No one wants to deal with puzzles like these, but they're often an unavoidable part of life and must be addressed, so we puzzle through them, working to fit the pieces together as best we can.

Incidentally, cognitive scientists say that one of the skills needed for doing jigsaw puzzles is the ability to do "mental rotation." This means you can rotate objects in your mind and see them from different perspectives. Not surprisingly, the ability to see things from different perspectives helps solve real-life puzzles too.

For me, every book I've set out to write has seemed like a real-life puzzle. I usually start with a general idea of what the final picture should look like, but I don't know how many pieces I'll need to fit together, only that the whole puzzle must be solved by the publisher's deadline.

A thornier puzzle arose when I once started a small business and naively took in someone I didn't know well—a friend of a friend—as an equal owner. We soon found we were mismatched. Solving that puzzle—separating ourselves, passing the business on to someone else, and getting on with other pursuits—took several difficult years. Hard as it was, I'll put that one in my gift shop because at least I learned never to repeat the same mistake.

What challenging puzzles have you had to solve, and can you be grateful for having met the challenge? Did the experience, difficult as it was, allow you to grow and gain wisdom? If so, you can make a place here for that very personal puzzle in your Gift Shop of Gratitude.

Gratitude

Gratitude

Gratitude

18

Ornaments: Reminders of Faith and Ritual

Many gift shops, no matter where they're located or the time of year, stock religious ornaments. Glass or plastic balls decorated with a winter or Christmas theme are made as decorations for Christmas trees. The Hamsa, in the shape of an open hand and symbolizing protection against evil, is an ornament popular with people of many religions, including Jews and Muslims.

Some ornaments can be creative. The gift shop at the US Supreme Court offers ornaments in the shape of a gavel and the scales of justice. The Rock & Roll Hall of Fame in Cleveland, Ohio, sells an ornament that says, "Peace, Music, Love," and another that shows a colorfully painted "hippie van" against a backdrop of vibrant, psychedelic colors. "A fun addition to your holiday decorations," says the Rock Hall, "a must for hippies old and new!"

Eighty percent of consumers in a survey planned in the current year to purchase new ornaments. The ornament industry generates billions of dollars in sales annually. One study found that an average-sized Christmas tree—about six and a half feet tall—typically will hold between 70 and 105 ornaments. On taller trees, up to nine or ten feet, there may be as many as 200.

The continuing appeal of religious ornaments is a reminder that faith, and faith-based traditions, can be an enduring source of meaning and comfort for many people. Thus, they have a well-deserved place in the Gift Shop of Gratitude.

One's faith may be something we're born into or something we choose; it may be an organized religion or a personal spiritual journey. Either way, we can be grateful for having it as an anchor. Over time, one's faith may wax and wane, but the core belief in God, or something greater than the self and the observable world, can give meaning to existence and, in hard times, be a rock.

Faith traditions and rituals can also be sources of strength and comfort. In practical terms, they can be like building blocks that help us organize the year, the week, and even the day into meaningful parts.

For me, I'm grateful for the weekly observance of the Sabbath, what Rabbi Abraham Joshua Heschel called a "sanctuary in time." Late Friday afternoon, I stop working—even if I'm in the middle of a chapter, like this one—and begin twenty-four hours of ritual, reflection, and rest. At dinner, we light Sabbath candles, recite blessings, and enjoy a relaxed meal with family and friends. The next morning at synagogue, we study a section of Torah (the first five books of the Hebrew Bible), enjoy lunch with other congregants, and in the afternoon enjoy a walk, a nap, or visit with friends—before the new week begins.

The influence of clergy—rabbis, priests, pastors, imams, and other spiritual leaders—can be another aspect of faith for which to be grateful. Their learning can be a source of wisdom and their counsel a source of comfort.

One category of religious leaders we often forget to acknowledge is military chaplains. Yet, thousands of veterans will attest to the sacrifices chaplains make for the well-being of the troops in their care.

What aspects of faith are you most grateful for? Have you endured trials during which your faith was a comfort and helped keep you from despair? Have spiritual leaders you've known been exceptional teachers or sources of inspiration or comfort? Which rituals have been meaningful to you and enriched your life?

What images would be on your ornaments?

Gratitude

Gratitude

Gratitude

19

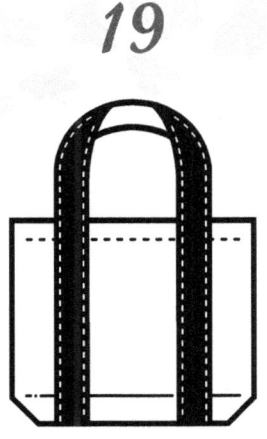

Tote Bags: The Things We Carry With Us

Totes—unfastened bags made of sturdy fabric with parallel handles—are a staple of gift shops. They're handy and reusable, and they also offer benefits similar to other gift shop items.

Like coffee mugs, the sides of tote bags can be a place for wise sayings. I saw one that says, "Grow Through What You Go Through." Like the brims of baseball caps, totes can be used to signal that you're part of a group or team, like the popular "I Heart National Public Radio" tote. And, as with T-shirts, with totes you can celebrate special places and events, like one that says, "Family Myrtle Beach Vacation 2024."

But one thing you can do with totes that you can't do with other gift shop items is carry things. This makes totes popular with travelers because we can always use an extra bag to carry stuff home.

I think it's smart that gift shops sell tote bags because then you've got a big bag to put everything else in that you buy there.

In a good-sized tote bag, I bet I could fit a lot of other gift shop items: a couple of coffee mugs, a baseball cap, a T-shirt or two, some scented candles, a deck of playing cards, matching shot glasses, souvenir spoons, maybe even a couple of bobbleheads. The only gift items that probably wouldn't fit would be a stuffed animal larger than a small teddy bear or a jigsaw puzzle if it's over 300 pieces.

This is the practical use of the tote bag: you can carry a lot in it.

But I include tote bags in the Gift Shop of Gratitude not for the physical "stuff" you can carry in it, but because tote bags remind us that, as we make our way through life—and as author Tim O'Brien taught in his brilliant book, *The Things They Carried*—we also carry intangible things.

Like memories.

We carry memories of childhood, of parents and grandparents, of the town and the homes we grew up in. Some of these memories—both good and bad—shaped our personalities, still influence our beliefs and behavior, and by themselves probably could fill a tote bag to the brim.

We carry our family's heritage, sometimes referred to as "roots." It's where we come from, and it's the stories, beliefs, and practices that earlier generations passed down to us. That my grandparents uprooted their lives to come to this country, that my dad and his brothers worked hard to start and succeed in business, and that they passed along to me 3,000-year-old Jewish traditions that anchor me, give my life meaning, and encourage me to explore and question, for all this that I carry, I'm filled with gratitude.

We carry responsibilities: to family, friends, community, and to our own beliefs. Sometimes we fulfill these; at other times we may forget or avoid them, but all the same, we carry them.

We carry values and ethical standards: from parents, faith traditions, and our own experience of living. Sometimes, in trying to live up to these values, we miss the mark, but even then, we can be grateful for having the values to aim for.

We carry regrets—I hope not enough to fill anyone's tote. Even Frank Sinatra, in his signature song, "My Way," admitted he had a few regrets. I've noticed that as the years pass, some regrets seem to diminish. But some remain. They're at the bottom of my tote, among the heavier items.

We carry hopes: for our children and grandchildren, and all who come after us, that they'll know love, that their lives will be fulfilling, their trials tolerable.

In some traditions, people may write a document, called an Ethical Will, in which they describe the values they've lived by, lessons learned, and hopes for the lives that their offspring will lead. It's an attempt to transmit ethical values from one generation to the next. Not only are they passing down their assets, but they are also conveying their beliefs.

This tote bag—indeed, the whole Gift Shop of Gratitude—is a kind of Ethical Will, letting those who come after us know the things for which we're most grateful.

What will you put into your tote bag? Memories, responsibilities, aspects of your heritage, regrets, hopes? I wouldn't worry about making the bag too full; the fuller you make it, the more will be there for future generations to unpack, understand, and remember you.

Gratitude

Gratitude

 Gratitude

20

Postcards: Glad I Was Here

The movie, *Having Wonderful Time*, was a 1938 romantic comedy adapted from a play of the same name. The title is a nod to the tradition of people on vacation sending postcards to family and friends with the cliched message, "Having wonderful time. Wish you were here!" (In fact, a later musical was entitled *Wish You Were Here*.)

Even in this digital age, the humble postcard survives. I can't think of a single gift shop I've seen that doesn't carry a rack of them. "Despite the sheer convenience of digital correspondence," observes Pen Heaven, a British-based seller of pens and journals, "traditional postcards still have a thriving fan base." To understand why, they asked young people what it is they like about postcards.

"There's something so organic about putting words on paper that you don't get with a computer screen," said one. Another, speaking of the "authenticity" of a handwritten note, said, "It feels far more personal." A person who likes receiving postcards said she enjoys "deciphering my friend's handwriting" and appreciates the effort her friend made "to find the postcard, buy stamps, write the message, and mail it."

Finally, and to me somewhat surprisingly, it turns out people like the space limitation set by a writing area only a few inches across. "You're able to offer glimpses into the adventure you're having but not give it all away," one person said. Noted another, "Writing a postcard means actually sitting down and thinking about what to say—not just typing the first thing that comes into your head—so that what comes out is a more detailed, special message."

And that is, indeed, the beauty of postcards. They let us send brief, but thoughtful and special messages to people we care about, and for that I give them the closing spot in the Gift Shop of Gratitude.

If you could write a postcard to those you've most treasured on this trip through life, to whom would you write, and what would be the message? It won't be "Having wonderful time. Wish you were here," because they were here, and it was their being here that helped you have a wonderful time.

Maybe you'd mention, briefly, some of the experiences, sights, opportunities, or challenges that gave life the most meaning and for which you're most grateful.

I can think of two postcards I'd write. Just for fun, I'd stick close to the classic formula of "Having a wonderful time" and so on.

The first would be a postcard to my three children; they'd have to pass it around. I'd say, "Sarah, Val, and Ben—you've made my life a wonderful time. I'm so grateful you were here."

In the second postcard, to my wife, Elisa, I'd turn the classic message around and say, "I wished you would be here, and my wish came true. Now, together, we're having a wonderful time."

What postcard messages will you write to the people you most treasure? You might mention the best sights you've seen on this trip through life and whatever allows you, looking back, to say, "Have had some wonderful times. So grateful I was here."

In the spaces, write your special postcard messages. No stamp required.

Gratitude

# Gratitude

Gratitude

Acknowledgments

First, I thank the Claude Monet house and gardens in Giverny, France, for blocking my wife, Elisa Kaplan Siegel, and me from leaving through the exit and instead insisting that we retrace our steps—in the rain—back through the gardens and the house to exit only through the gift shop. Without that bit of annoyance, I likely never would have started thinking about gift shops or their metaphorical meaning.

Thank you to Julie Pfitzinger of Twin Cities PBS's *Next Avenue*; and to Paul Ericson and Smriti Jacob of the *Rochester Beacon*, my hometown paper, for running the articles where I first expressed the ideas later developed in this book.

Literary agent Nick Mullendore of the Vertical Ink Agency and I reconnected at just the right moment. Nick's been a pleasure to work with, and I'm grateful for his good advice and perseverance.

To Gilles Dana, founder and president of G&D Media, for seeing the potential in this project, I offer sincere thanks. Ditto to G&D staff who helped in the book's swift creation: Evan Litzenblatt, Meghan Day Healey, and Ellen Goldberg. And thanks to David Rheinhardt for enhancing this book with his charming illustrations.

Warm thanks to Sandra Wendel, my editor, who saw from the beginning the book's potential and at every step of the process has made it a better and more meaningful work.

To Rabbi David A. Katz, thank you for those early discussions that helped me better understand the gift shop metaphor, for your learned and moving Meditation on Gratitude that serves as this book's foreword, and for our continuing friendship—now more than sixty years strong.

Acknowledgments

I began these acknowledgments by describing the experience Elisa and I had at the Monet house and gardens in France. From the beginning of this project—indeed, starting with the train ride back to Paris when I first said, "You know, you could also see a gift shop as a metaphor"—Elisa has been my sounding board, my first reader and editor, and my chief encourager. Since that trip, she's also become my wife, for which I'm so grateful—but to adequately express that would take a whole other book.

And, finally, to my grandchildren—Maya, Andrew, Talia, Asaf, Mollie, and Yael—and those yet to come, may your gifts and your gratitude always be abundant.

About the Author

Peter Lovenheim is an author and journalist whose articles and essays have appeared in the *New York Times*, *New York* magazine, *Los Angeles Times*, *Parade*, *Politico*, *The Forward*, *AARP Magazine*, and *Washington Post*. He is Washington Correspondent for the *Rochester Beacon*, an online source of news and commentary for his hometown of Rochester, New York.

His previous books of nonfiction include *The Attachment Effect* (2018), an exploration of how early bonds with parents shape personality throughout life; *In the Neighborhood: The Search for Community on an American Street, One*

Sleepover at a Time (2012), winner of a Barnes & Noble Discover Award and the First Annual Zócalo Public Square Book Prize; and *Portrait of a Burger as a Young Calf* (2002), a firsthand attempt to understand the food chain.

Lovenheim holds a degree in journalism from Boston University and in law from Cornell Law School. He splits his time between Rochester, NY, and Washington, DC.

Rabbi David A. Katz, who has served Reform congregations coast-to-coast, is a member of the Central Conference of American Rabbis.

www.ingramcontent.com/pod-product-compliance
Lightning Source LLC
Chambersburg PA
CBHW061736070526
44585CB00024B/2688